BROCKHAMPTON PRESS

Picture Reference book of CASTLES AND FORTIFICATIONS

Consultant Editor: Boswell Taylor
Research and illustrations: Leslie Marshall MSIA

CONTENTS

TODAY, castles are tourist attractions. Originally they were built as massive machines designed for ruling and for fighting. The ancient civilizations of the Egyptians, Hittites, Assyrians and Romans were skilled in the art of building fortifications. The Great Wall of China was begun before 200 BC, but, in Europe, castles are mainly identified with the Middle Ages. In these war-troubled years the castle flourished with the age of chivalry, of knight and archer, and died with the onslaught of artillery. Against lance and arrow, the castle was a refuge. Cannon turned it into a trap. At their peak, castles were military bases for offensive warfare. Crusaders built them as stepping stones of faith to the Holy Land. Castles were also the homes and edifices of feudal power, from which lords and kings dominated the surrounding land. Now, they belong to legend and folklore. They have their place in our heritage; in our stories of armoured knights rescuing maids in distress, in tales of courage and mighty deeds and, also, in records of medieval savagery and cruel warfare.

Early fortifications

manuscript by Marcus Vitruvius Pollio, Roman architect 1st century BC, with English translation

[Moreover, towns are not to be planned squa with projecting angles, but on the round, so t the enemy be seen from several sides. For wh angles run out, defence is difficult, because th angle defends the enemy rather than the towr men. But I think the width of the wall should so made that armed men meeting one another above can pass without hindrance. Then, in th width, through-timbers of charred olive wood should be put very frequently, in order that b fronts of the wall, being tied together by these timbers, as though by pins, may have everlast strength. For such timber cannot be injured b decay or weather or age; even when it is cover with soil or placed in water, it remains unimp and useful for ever. And so not only the city but the substructures, and those dividing walls which are made to be of the thickness of fortifications, when united in this manner, wi quickly be decayed. The distances between th towers are so to be made that one is not furth from another than a bowshot; so that if a tow besieged anywhere, then, by 'scorpions' and o missile engines from the towers right and left, enemy may be thrown back. And also opposit lower part of the towers, the wall is to be divi by intervals as wide as a tower; and these inte opposite the interior parts of the towers shall joined with planks. These, however, are not to fixed with iron nails. For if the enemy occupi any part of the wall, the defenders shall cut th down, and if they manage it quickly, they will suffer the enemy to penetrate the rest of the towers and wall, unless he is willing to throw h self headlong. The towers therefore are to be r round or polygonal ..

reconstructed section of the walls of Troy of the Mycenean Age, c.1500 BC, with steep batter up to 20 feet high. It shows the offsets between the sections

slightly exaggerated plan of Troy, showing the straight panels of wall set to form the curve required. This would be stronger than a continuous curve

siege of an Assyrian 9th-century BC city, based on a sculpture from the Palace of Ashurnasirpal II

From prehistoric times man has lived with fear: fear of attack upon himself and his possessions. He has been in fear of the elements, the lightning that could kill in a flash or the forest fire that consumed all. He has feared wild animals. But most of all he has feared attacks made by other men. He has set up defences against these enemies. At first they were crude fences manufactured from the surrounding trees, or fires that blazed defiance at the opening of his cave. Lake people were

ɪ wooden *pluteus,* according to /egetius, a late Roman writer on nilitary affairs. It moved on :hree wheels

△ Mai Dun (often called Maiden Castle) in Dorset; a Celtic variant of the walled town. The hillside falling away on all sides has been sculpted into a number of obstacles and the main entrance, to the right, offers a series of 'breakwaters' against the incoming tide of an attack

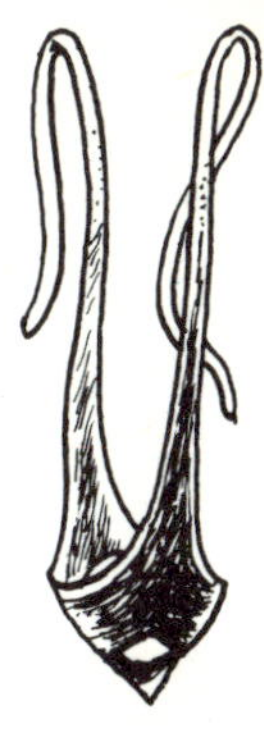

hand sling. Slings were used in the defence of Maiden Castle

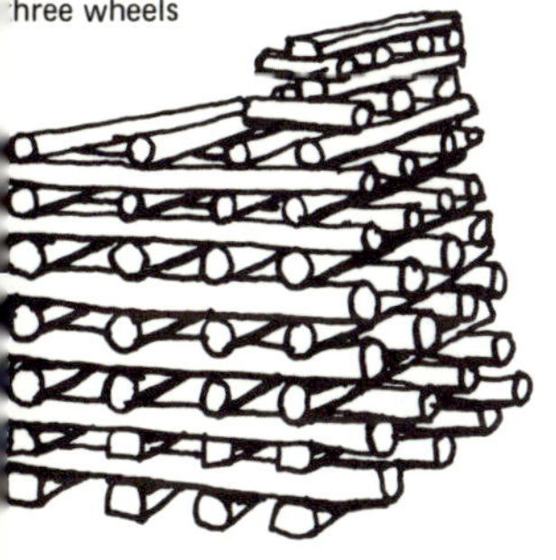

ancient walls were often of timber filled with rubble or earth then faced with stones. Such walls would be proof against battering-rams

Great Wall of China, usually regarded as having been built 246-210 BC

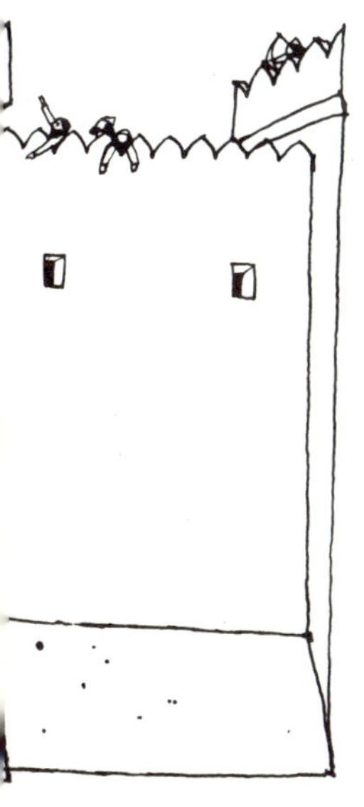

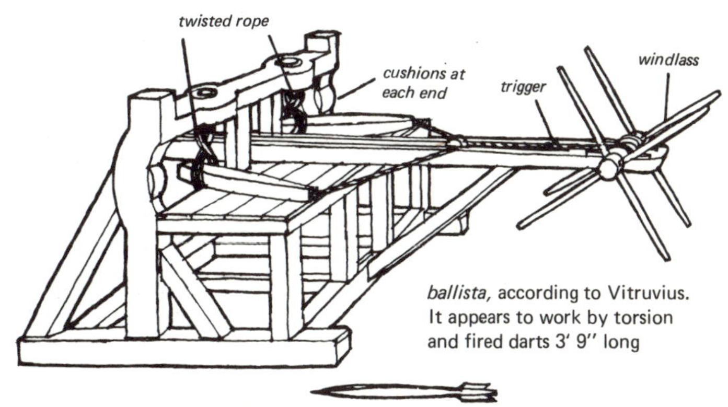

ballista, according to Vitruvius. It appears to work by torsion and fired darts 3′ 9″ long

protected by the surrounding water. As man left the natural protection of cave and forest den, he felt the need for greater protection. He built walls to guard himself and his home. A tribe surrounded the whole village with a fence. As villages grew into cities, the fences became city walls. Many cities still possess their city walls. But powerful men had their own fortified home — and this was the castle.

centurial stone found at Cawfields Mile castle of the force commanded by Valerius Maximus on Hadrian's Wall. Each legion allotted its centuries a stretch of the wall. They worked on a leapfrog basis, signing off at the end of their allotted stretch with an inscription such as this

Roman and Byzantine

Chester's Fort, one of the nine forts built along Hadrian's Wall. It garrisoned up to 500 men, which included cavalry. Roman cavalry could travel 70 miles in 24 hours. Such units would give flexibility to the defence of the Wall ▷

map showing Hadrian's Wall, Antonine Wall, roads, forts and signal stations

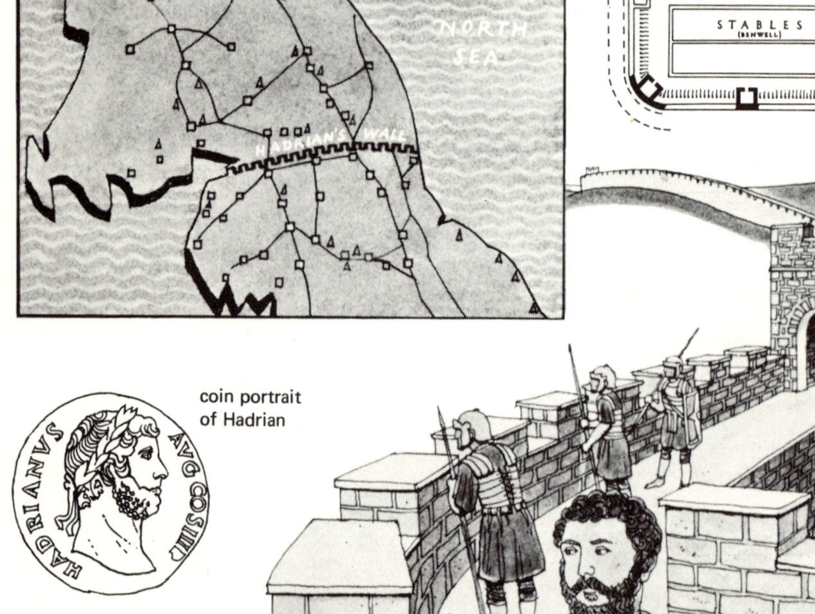

coin portrait of Hadrian

surprise attack on Hadrian's Wall

Military engineers studied the art of siegecraft. A school devoted to the subject was even founded by 200 BC on the island of Rhodes. Engineers exploited their craft in Alexandria, Byzantium and the Arabian countries. The Eastern civilizations flourished and died, but the well-built fortifications often remained. Invading Romans learned from these remains and developed their own techniques. The simplest form was the earthwork rampart with its ditches that

nineteenth-century engraving of the Porta Nigra Roman gateway c.AD 300, at Trier, West Germany

the gates of San Sebastiano in the Aurelian Wall, Rome ▽

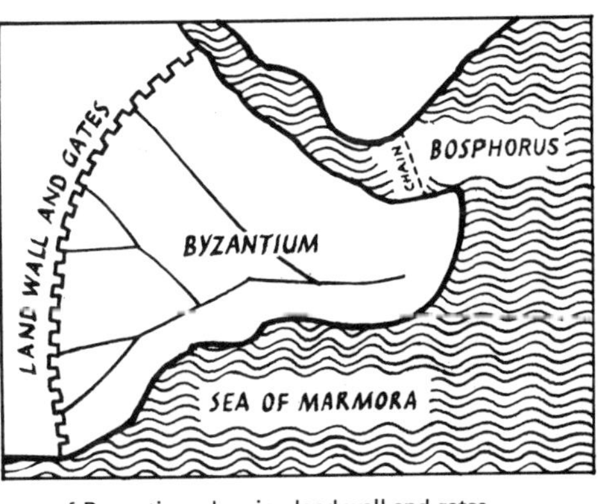

map of Byzantium showing land wall and gates

land walls of Byzantium, begun in AD 413 as defence against the Ostrogoths and ▽ the Huns. Byzantium has also been called Constantinople and is now known as Istanbul

nstantine Paleologus, t Byzantine Emperor, o died 1453 defending e walls of Byzantium ainst the Turks

surrounded the military camp or *castrum.* Permanent settlements had stone ramparts strong enough and thick enough to contain towers. Against these fortifications four main types of siegecraft were developed: mining, ramming, escalading and attacking with projectiles, such as the *petraria* and *ballista.* The aim in mining was to weaken the foundations of the walls. Counter-measures were developed to defy these attacks.

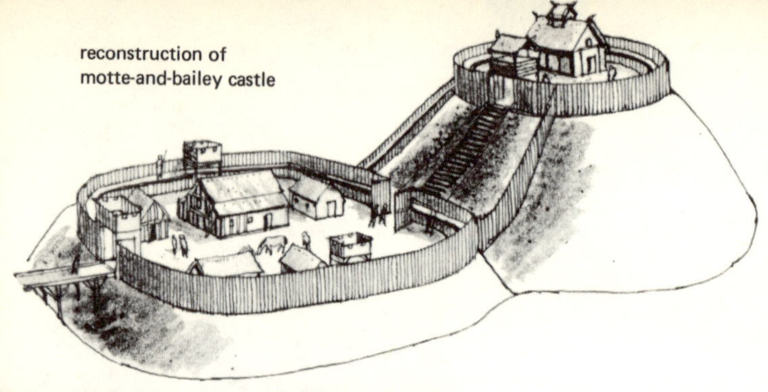
reconstruction of motte-and-bailey castle

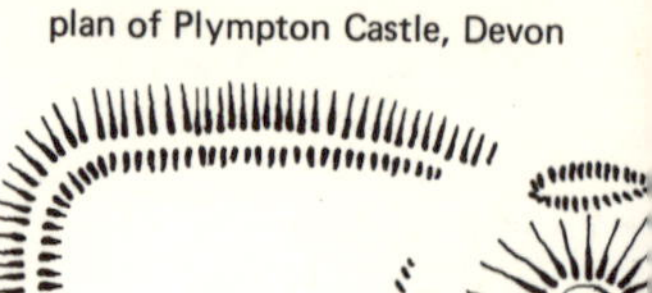
plan of Plympton Castle, Devon

Motte-and-bailey castles

motte-and-bailey castle at Pickering, Yorkshire

from the Bayeux Tapestry; the Castle of Dinan

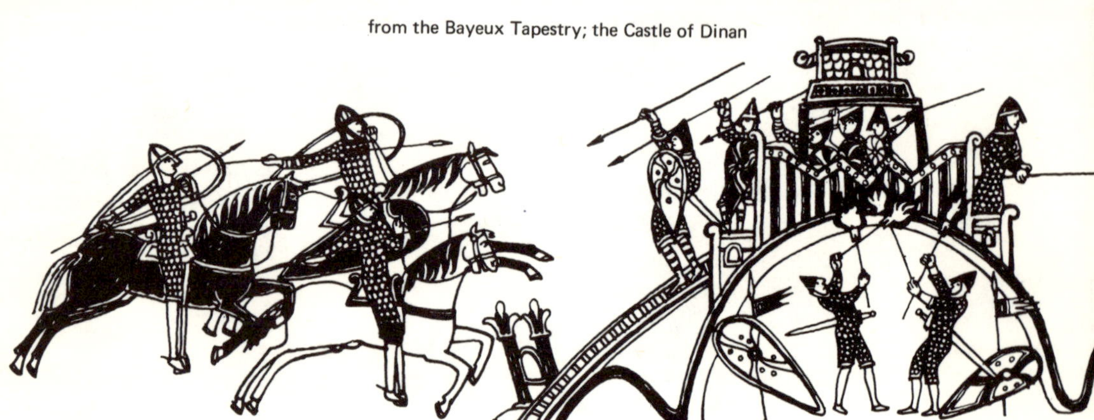
a continuous narrative showing: the attack on the castle; the setting fire to the castle by knights

William I conquered England at the Battle of Hastings. He maintained his grip on the country through his castles 'which were built far and wide throughout the land, oppressing the unhappy people' *(Anglo-Saxon Chronicle).* The original Norman castle was the motte-and-bailey construction. As it consisted mainly of wood and earth, it was cheap and simple to build. The motte was an artificial hillock on which was constructed a tower. The bailey was a large outer court lying

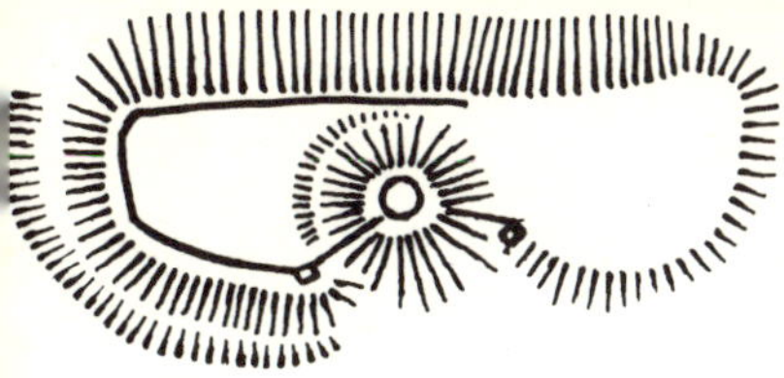

plan of Arundel Castle, Sussex

Windsor Castle. The motte together with the two baileys are clearly seen underlying the castle plan

the surrender of the keys

wooden stave church c. 1150 at Borgund in Western Norway; of a similar style of construction to the castle of Dinan

at a lower level than the motte. The summit and base of the motte, and the bailey, were surrounded by palisades. The excavations left a ditch which surrounded the whole structure and served as an additional protection. The bailey was large enough to contain barns and storehouses, as well as the cookhouse. In some instances advantage was taken of physical features such as outcrops of rock. These castles dominated the countryside for more than a hundred years.

Rochester keep.
In 1215 King John's men undermined one of the square corner towers and broke into the keep

Keeps

shell keep, Gisors, Normandy, 12th century

Restormel Castle in Cornwall, 11th century. In some places, the wooden palisade round the summit of the motte was replaced by a circular stone wall. This was a shell keep. Inside the shell, the old wooden tower was demolished to make room for buildings of stone

For centuries, from the ninth century onwards, feudalism was the social system in Europe. Land and rights were held by a vassal in return for allegiance to his lord. The power of the overlord was demonstrated in the strength and domination of the castle in which he lived. From the wooden tower and palisade fence developed the stone keeps, ramparts and moats of the feudal castle. Square keeps, or donjons, had advantages over the wooden mottes. They could be built

reconstruction of a mid-12th-century keep. Thick walls contain recesses and mural chambers. Some of these chambers are garderobes, others sleeping places

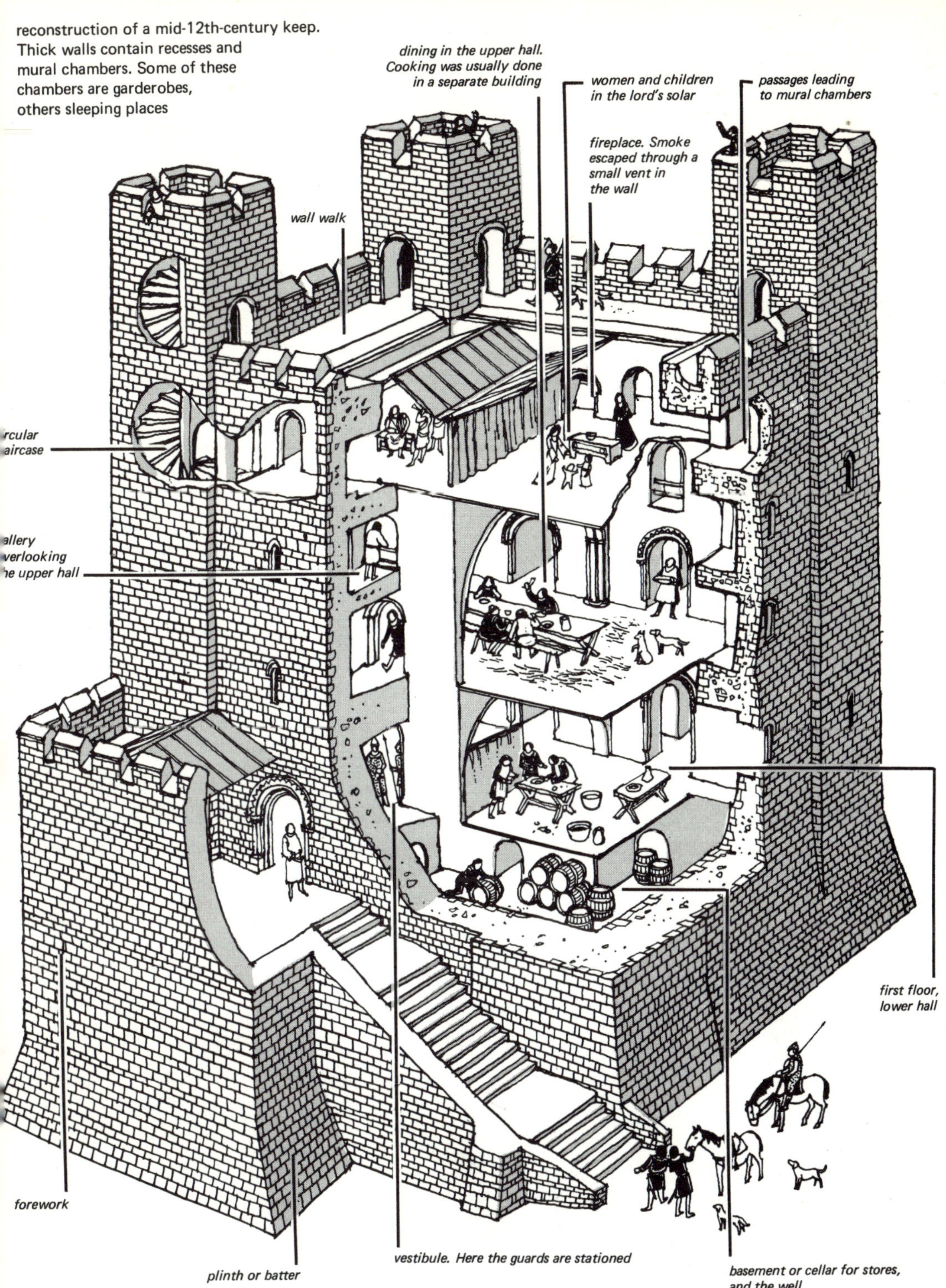

higher. They could not catch fire. They gave an impression of strength. But they had the disadvantage of limiting the field of fire, and they could be mined. Polygonal towers and round keeps were built to offset these disadvantages.

Gradually these were replaced by shell keeps, which were hollow fortresses built round a central courtyard. By the 12th century the circular keep and wall tower were common all over Europe.

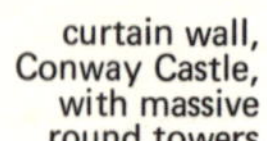
curtain wall, Conway Castle, with massive round towers

Curtain walls

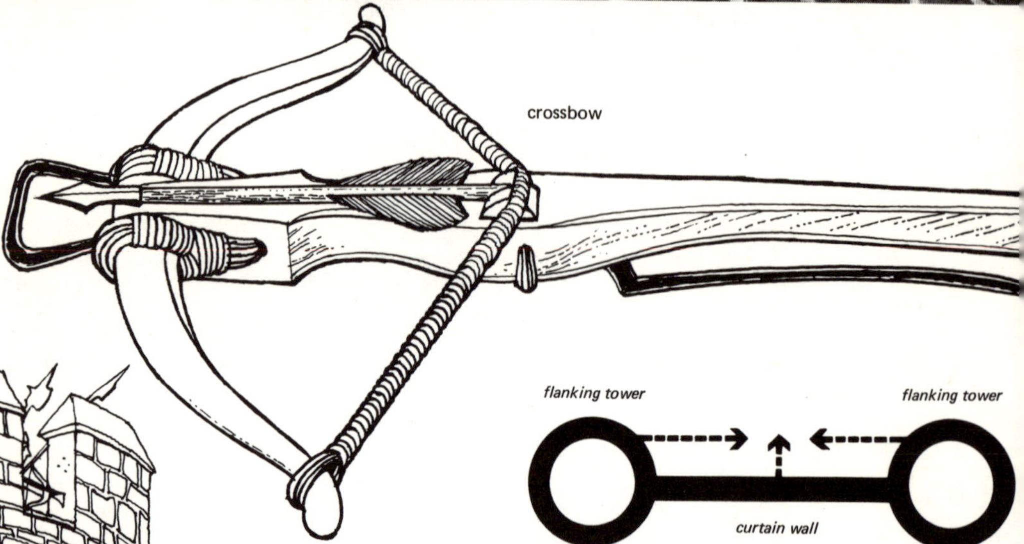

crossbow

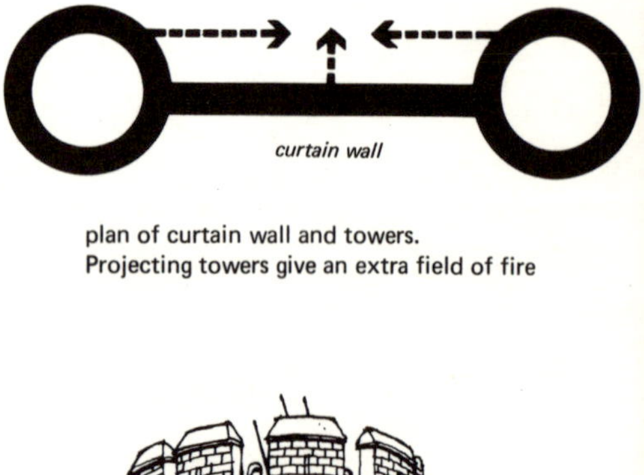

flanking tower

flanking tower

curtain wall

plan of curtain wall and towers. Projecting towers give an extra field of fire

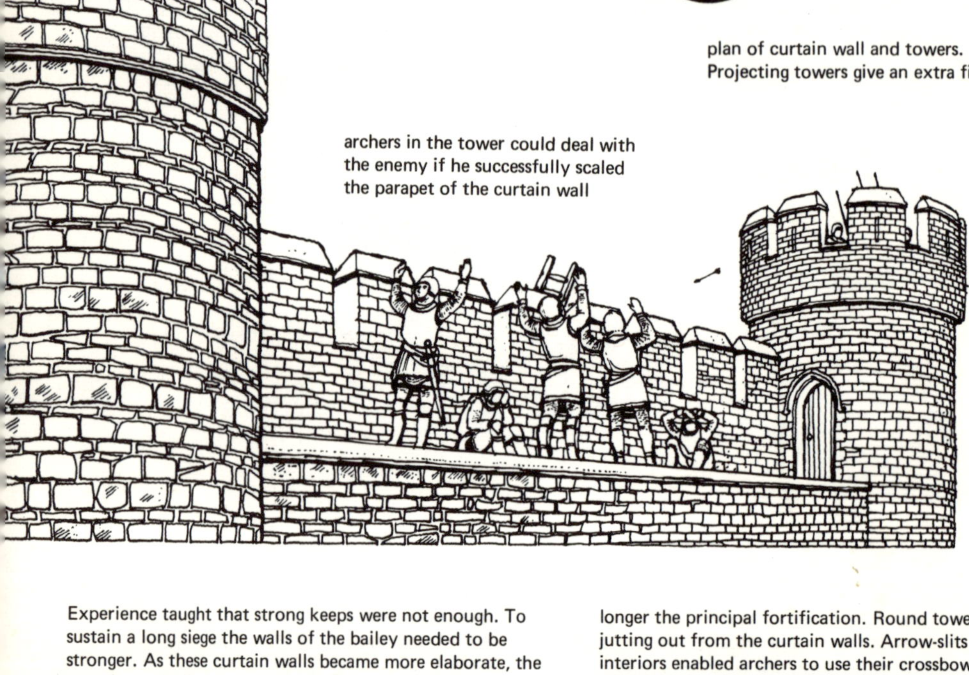

archers in the tower could deal with the enemy if he successfully scaled the parapet of the curtain wall

Experience taught that strong keeps were not enough. To sustain a long siege the walls of the bailey needed to be stronger. As these curtain walls became more elaborate, the great keep declined, until by the 13th century it was no longer the principal fortification. Round towers were built, jutting out from the curtain walls. Arrow-slits with splayed interiors enabled archers to use their crossbows without providing too obvious a target. In addition, for further

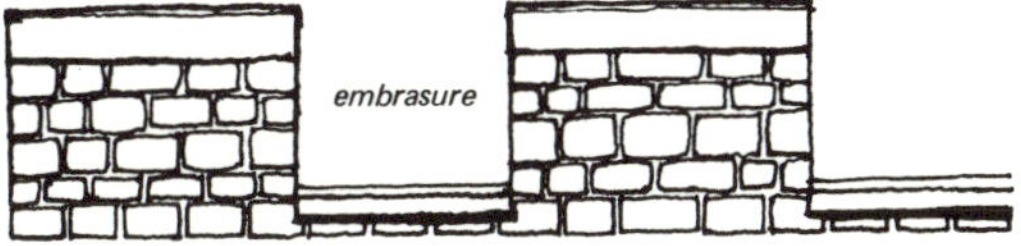

wooden shutters

machicolated parapet

four types of arrow-slit

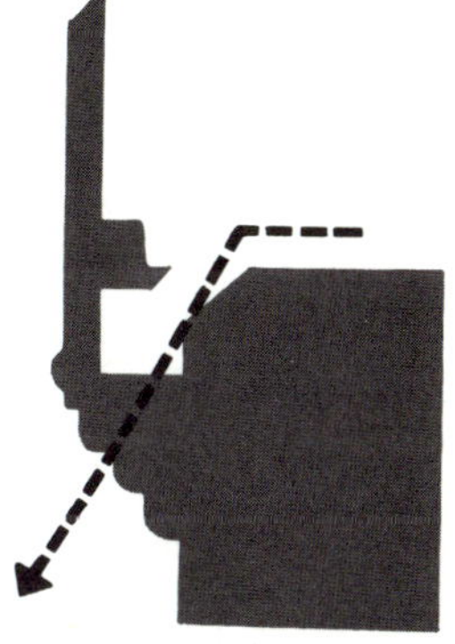

cross-section showing
missile path

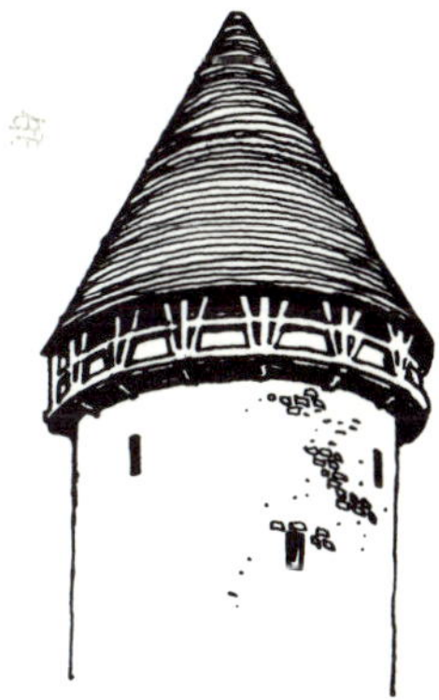

conical roofed tower
with wooden hoarding,
Heidenreichstein, Austria

south curtain wall at Angers, France.
Note the batter (proof against mining)

Framlingham Castle;
a castle without a keep

protection, the embattled parapets had wooden shutters. Later, wooden hoardings, built to project from the parapets, enabled the defenders to throw down stones and other missiles upon their attackers. When these became permanent, the gaps for the missile throwers became known as machicolations, and the rampart as a machicolated parapet. Castles were not only for defence, but also garrisons: the bases for attack.

Warwick Castle showing barbican

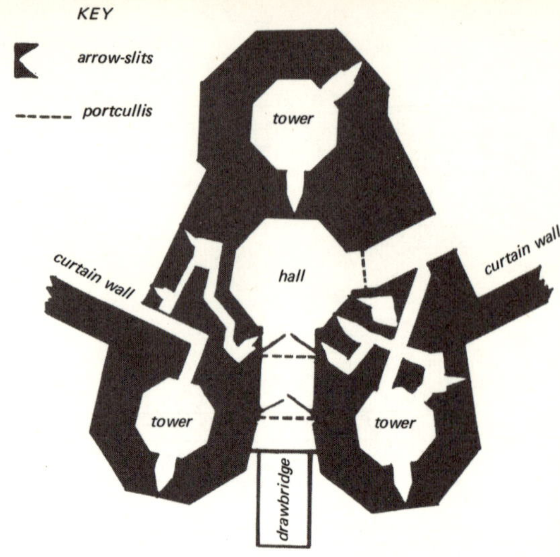

Denbigh, a three-tower gatehouse

Gatehouses and moats

gatehouse, Saltwood, Kent 1383

Bodiam Castle, gatehouse side, showing moat

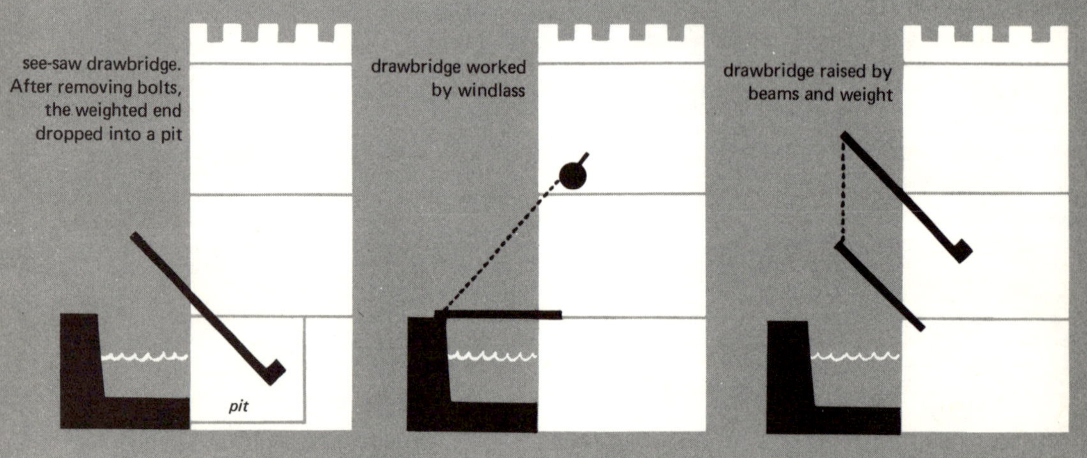

An obvious weakness in the curtain walls could be the gateway; the gates that opened to let the garrison out could be breached to let the attackers in. Aware of this, military engineers built stronger and bigger gatehouses that became forts in themselves. The approach across the moat was usually made over a wooden bridge. This could be raised against the gateway to make a second door. This drawbridge could be raised by chains. The alternative was a swing bridge balanced

Harlech Castle.
The gatehouse from the courtyard. Designed as the constable's residence, it had seven sets of machicolations, which would allow missiles to be rained down from the first floor into the passage

plan of Bodiam Castle with approach to gatehouse

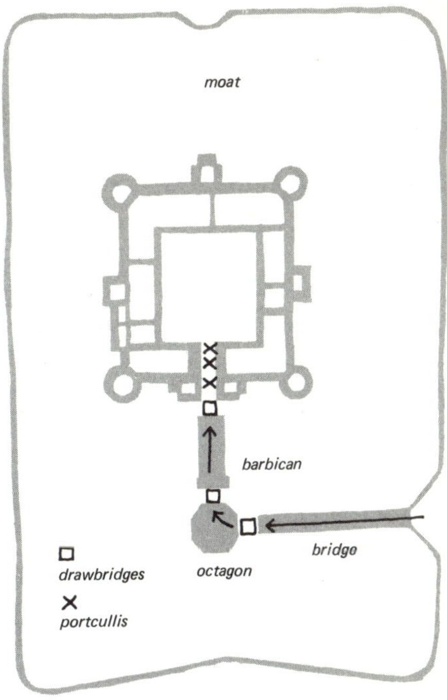

entrance gate and portcullis at Bodiam Castle (National Trust property)

portcullis mechanism above the gate leading to ▽ the Bloody Tower in the Tower of London

gatehouses were sometimes stormed after the gateway had been jammed with a cart, so that the gates could not be closed nor the portcullis lowered. This method was used to capture Edinburgh Castle in 1314

by counterweights. A portcullis, a free-drop door shod with iron spikes, could be rattled down from above. To give added strength, an outwork, called the barbican, was built. This fortress acted as the first line of defence in an attack. It was sometimes built into the gatehouse itself; or it might be an extension or even sited on the outside of the moat. Great ingenuity was shown in the placing of arrow-slits to provide the best field of fire.

MOAT
WELL
RIVER CLWYD
MOAT

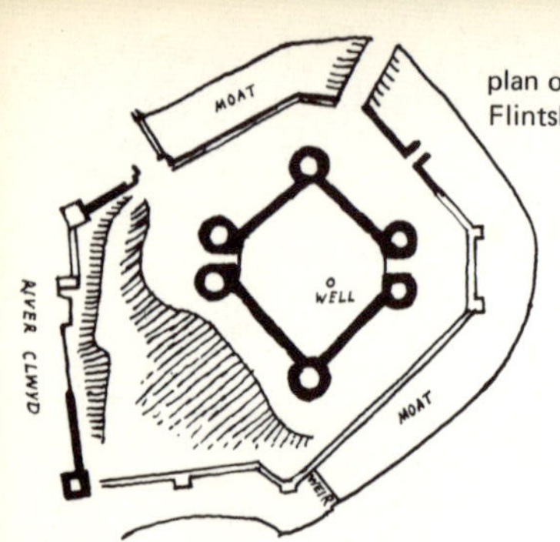

plan of Rhuddlan Castle, Flintshire, built 1277-81

Beaumaris Castle, Anglesey, seen from the air. Built 1295-1330. Loop-holes in the outer wall permitted archers to fire at the same time as the men above and a passage in the thickness of the curtain wall allowed defenders to move from one tower to another

▽

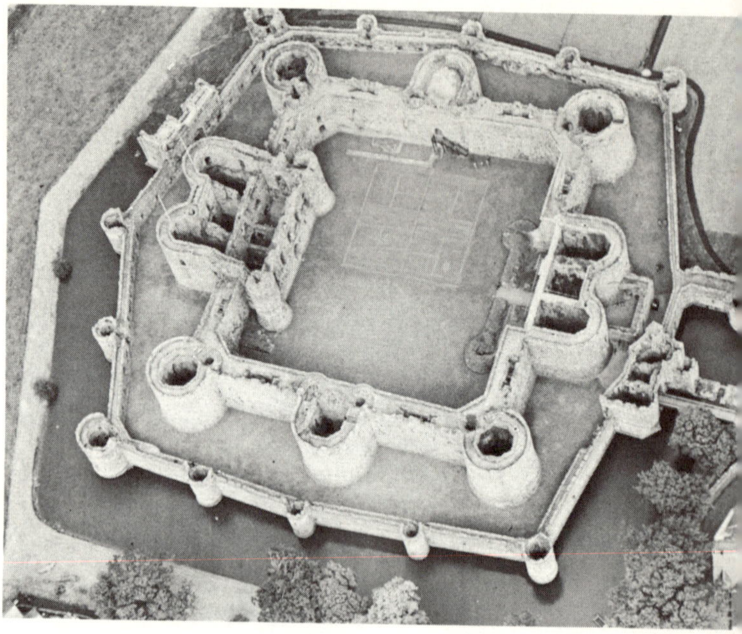

Concentric castles

Beaumaris
Caernaervon
Conway
Rhuddlan
Flint
Harlech
Aberystwyth
Builth

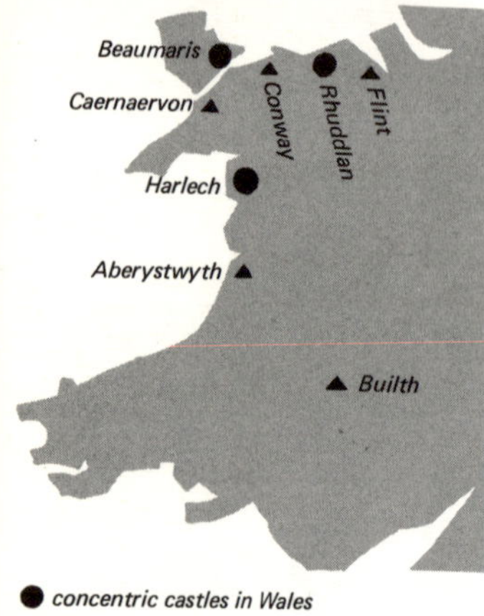

◁ Edwardian castles in Wales

● *concentric castles in Wales*

▲ *other castles built by Edward I*

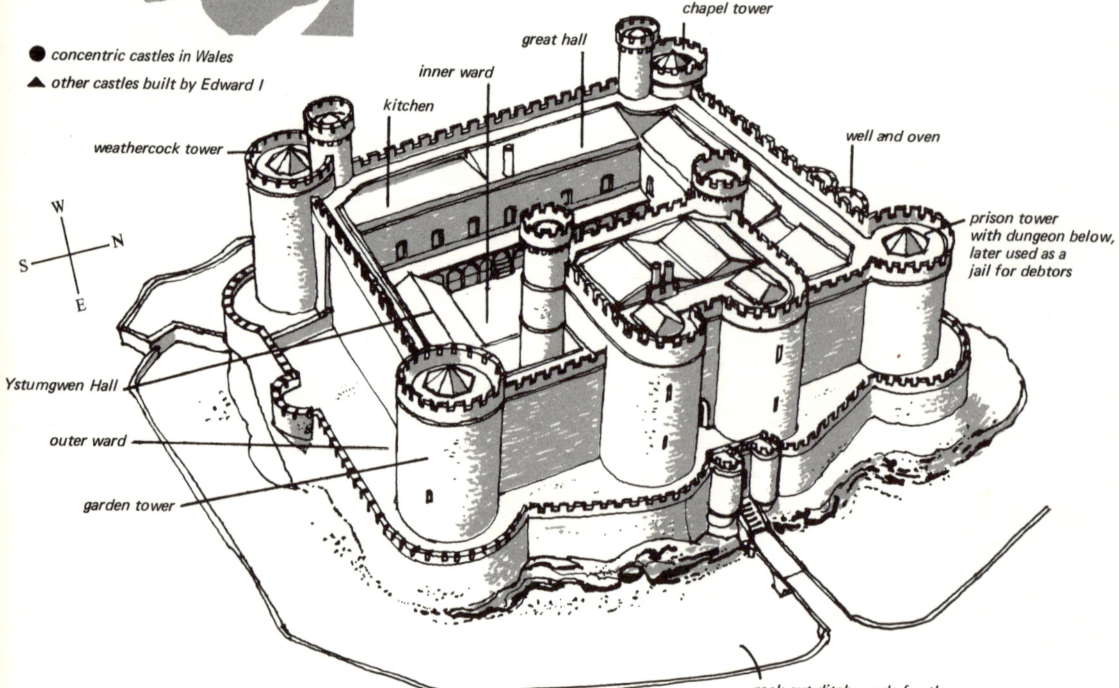

chapel tower
great hall
inner ward
kitchen
well and oven
weathercock tower
W
N
S
E
prison tower with dungeon below, later used as a jail for debtors
Ystumgwen Hall
outer ward
garden tower
rock-cut ditch, made for the sum of £205.17.1½d in 1285

Harlech Castle, Wales, built 1283-9

From the 5th century the Byzantines had built their fortifications with concentric walls. The outer wall was lower than the inner wall. This enabled the defenders to fire over the heads of those below. Crusaders became well aware of the value of concentric walls. When they returned home, they built the idea into their own castles. Krak des Chevaliers in Syria, Beaumaris in Anglesey, and the Tower of London are good examples of the concentric castle. Not only were these

Rhuddlan Castle, Wales. An immense inner wall was strengthened by round towers and an outer curtain, which was lower and less powerful

the land walls of Byzantium

Harlech Castle, the gatehouse approached from the town. The gatehouse is so mighty that it can be called a keep-gatehouse. Its defences include four great towers, two outward and two inward, with the passage between supplied with sets of doors, two portcullises and numerous murder-holes in the ceiling. The gatehouse at Harlech could hold out when the rest of the castle had been taken

knight of the time of Edward I

Harlech Castle as it may have looked in the Middle Ages

well-sited castles almost impregnable against frontal attack. They could withstand surprise sorties with their several lines of defence. They did not require large garrisons. Small bodies of defenders could withstand attacks from armies for weeks and even months. Food, drink and entertainment were available within the castle walls. They were also, geometrically and aesthetically, beautiful. With the concentric castle the high point of castle building was reached.

Life in the castle

pitcher, 13th century

cooking pot of bronze, 14th century, and, right, cook's flesh-hook

castle hall at Oakham

although much restored, the castle kitchen and its great ▷ fireplace at Marksburg in Germany must have looked much like this in medieval times

noble and lady, 1395

when a noble and his lady prepared to leave one of their castles in order to visit another, travelling arrangements were undertaken by the marshal. Furniture was taken with them

The basic needs were few: a great hall for communal living, a separate chamber for the lord and his family, and adequate storage space. In addition to its use as a fortress, the castle was a home for many people, an inn on occasions for travelling officials and nobility, and even a court. While there had to be a constant replenishment of supplies, stocks had to be maintained to face a siege. The lord of the castle was frequently absent, and then the lady or the castellan, the

garderobe or stone privy at Gravensteen, Ghent, Belgium

hawking scene from *Queen Mary's Psalter,* early 14th century. Note that the two women are riding astride; the hawk has already fastened on one of the ducks while the man on foot is ready to recall it with the lure

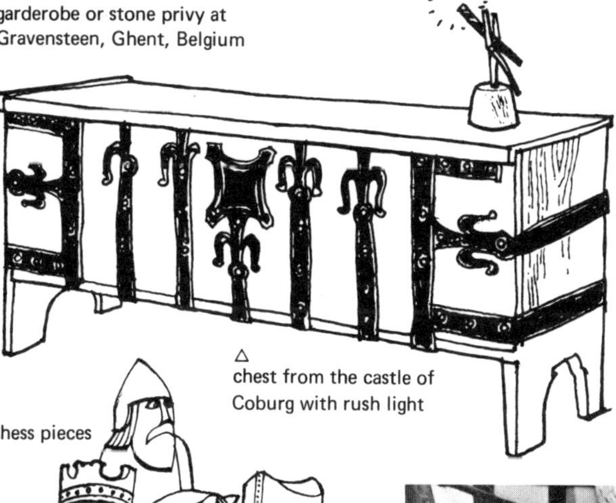

△ chest from the castle of Coburg with rush light

window seat at Chinon

chess pieces

castle well, worked by a donkey, at Carisbrooke Castle

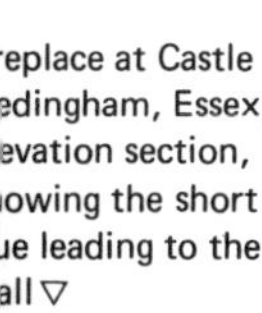

'eplace at Castle edingham, Essex; evation section, owing the short ue leading to the all ▽

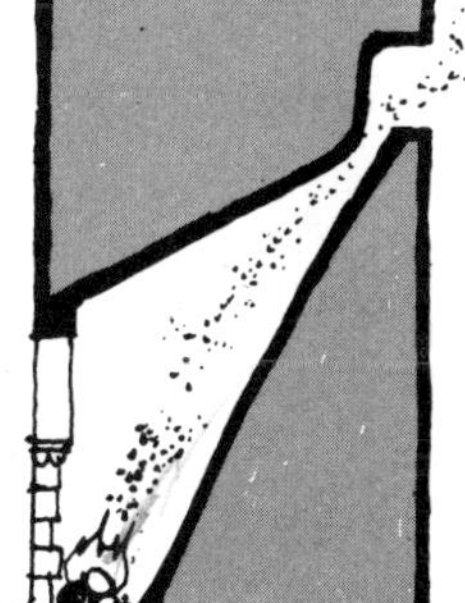

lord's deputy, was in charge. In addition to the castellan, the chief officers were the constable, the butler and the steward. In varying degrees of importance came the marshal, the knights, the clerks, and then the armourer, head groom, falconer, chief huntsman, and farrier. Furniture was limited to chests, beds and benches, with rare chairs. Troubadours entertained with songs. Other entertainments were chess and dancing, hunting and hawking.

reducing timber to planks

carpenters at work using adzes

Building

Work done	*Labour**	*Time 1283-1287*	*Cost*
22 towers 3 gates 1,400 yards of curtain wall 50 feet high surrounding ditch	170 masons 90 quarriers 28 carpenters 24 smiths 520 labourers 26 admin. staff 858 **figures based on Harlech labour force*	40 months (April to November each year)	£19,000 (a huge figure in the 13th century)

Conway Castle, Wales, begun under the architect James St George in 1283

Castle of Coca, Spain, constructed by Moslem workers (Mudejars) for the Archbishop o Seville. Brick-built with embrasures for cannon and gunloops

The site was of major importance. It had to be a natural stronghold, preferably a rocky peak or spur. It had to command an important route, or a city or a river. A good water supply was essential, both for the moat and for the kitchens. The surrounding lands must be able to supply food and labour, and pay for the running costs of the castle. The mobilization of huge supplies of material and manpower was the responsibility of the master mason. A large labour force

âteau Gaillard, built on a spur

Loarre Castle, Spain, built on a rocky peak

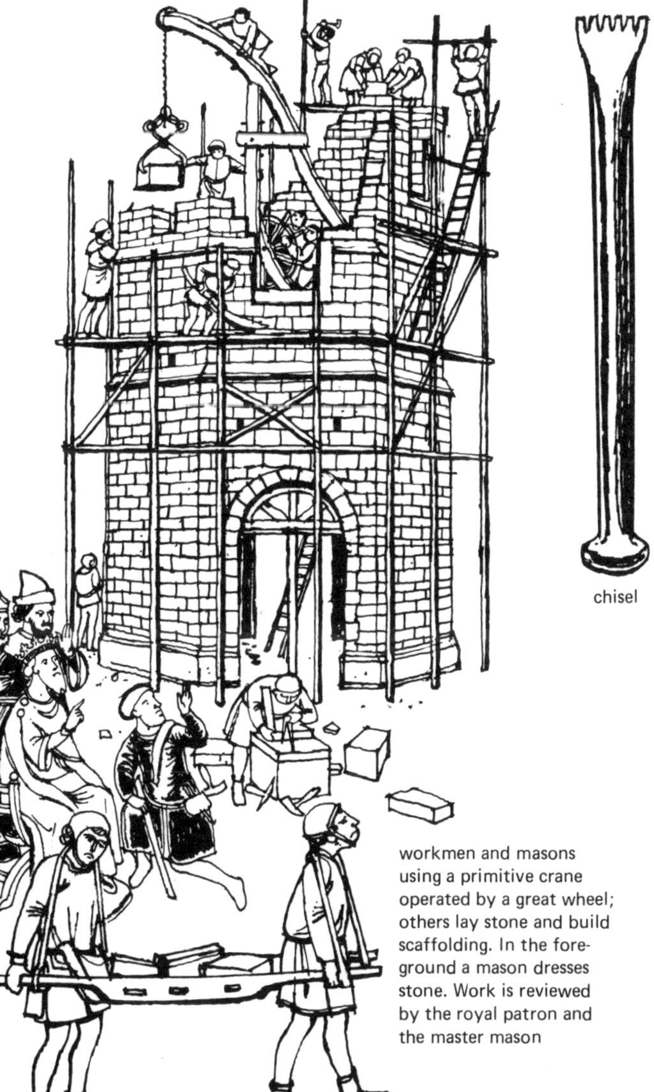

chisel

lifting techniques, using wheel and pulley, 15th century

workmen and masons using a primitive crane operated by a great wheel; others lay stone and build scaffolding. In the foreground a mason dresses stone. Work is reviewed by the royal patron and the master mason

13th-century French manuscript showing windlass and pulley

was required, made up of masons, quarriers, carpenters, smiths, clerks and unskilled labour. Sometimes pressed into labour, and often working at distances from their homes, the workers were submitted to rigorous discipline. Usually the work had to be done at speed and behind a temporary palisade. The foundations of the main curtain wall were laid first, and the walls and towers built to a reasonable height: The residential quarters were the last to be finished.

◁ battering-ram with a metal ram's hea
Battering-rams were usually trees cu
down on site and roughly trimmed;
effective against gates and corners o
square towers

Besieging a castle

penthouse, for giving cover to battering-ram parties and miners

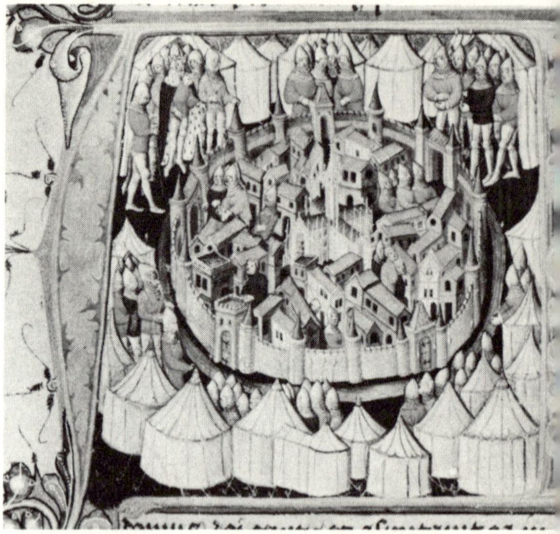

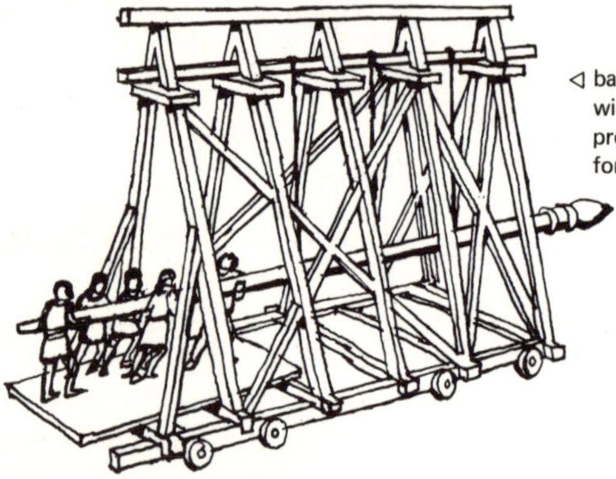

beleaguered city, from a 15th-century manuscript

◁ battering-ram, without its protective cladding, for reducing walls

ballista, worked by tension; note the traverse gear. These could be mounted on huge towers

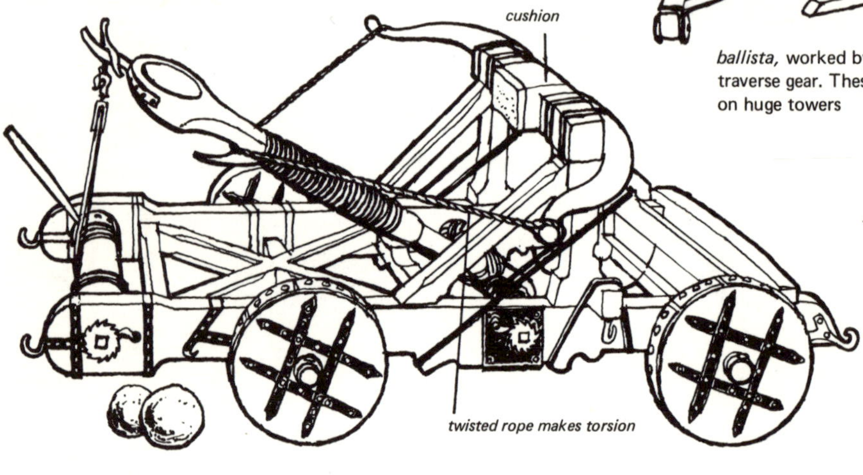

cushion

twisted rope makes torsion

◁ mangonel, worked by torsion.
This machine, however, incorporates tension to
it extra range. Mangonel
would not work well in
weather

The easiest way to besiege a castle was to squat in front of it and starve the occupants into surrender. Garrisons might surrender because they lacked manpower. They might lack work, food or ammunition. But it was the fall in the morale of the garrison that was the usual reason for the downfall of the castle. The defenders were worn out by constant vigilance, anxiety about the intentions of the attackers, and, most of all, by the sense of blockade. They appeared to be

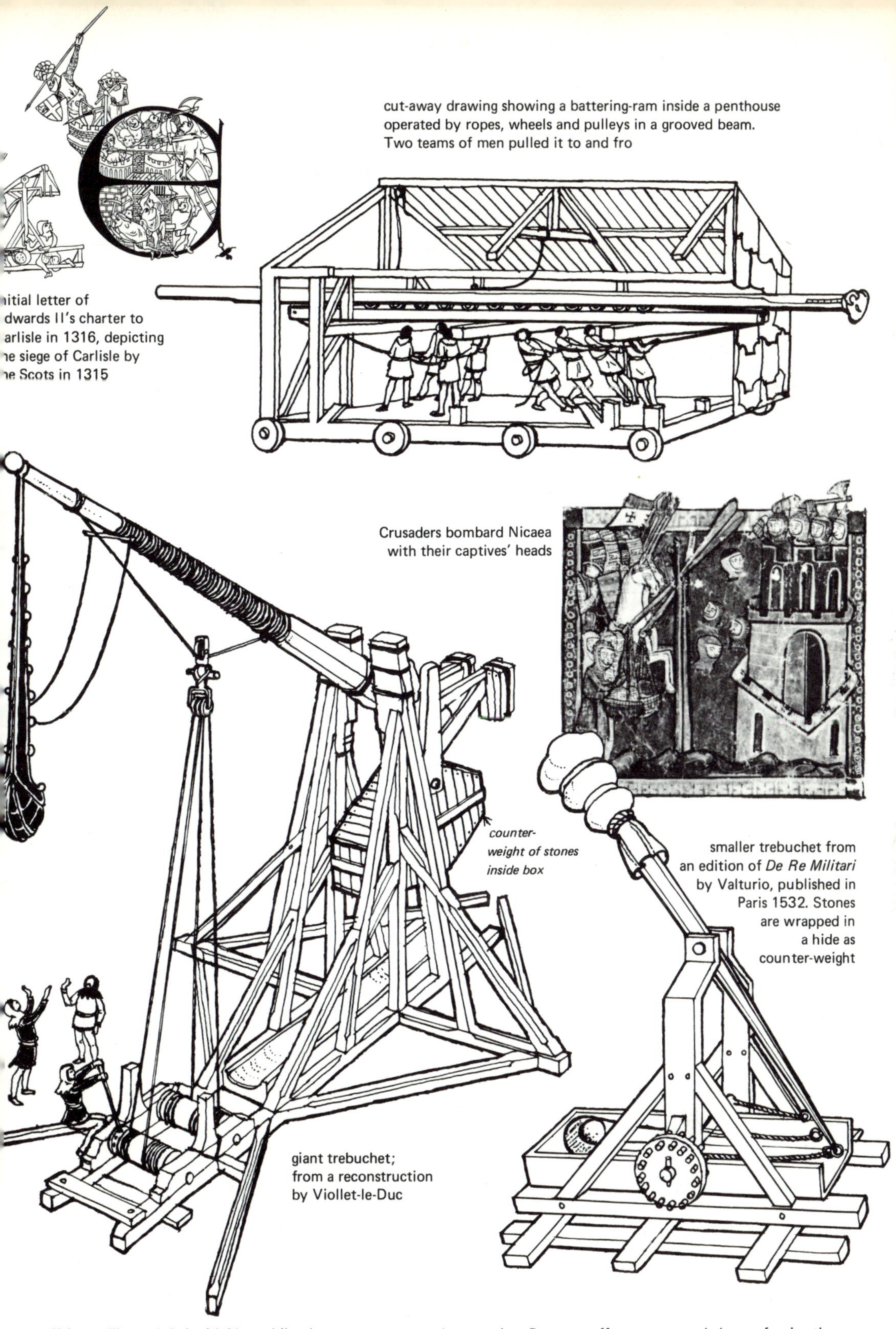

ıitial letter of
dwards II's charter to
arlisle in 1316, depicting
ıe siege of Carlisle by
ıe Scots in 1315

cut-away drawing showing a battering-ram inside a penthouse operated by ropes, wheels and pulleys in a grooved beam. Two teams of men pulled it to and fro

Crusaders bombard Nicaea with their captives' heads

smaller trebuchet from an edition of *De Re Militari* by Valturio, published in Paris 1532. Stones are wrapped in a hide as counter-weight

giant trebuchet; from a reconstruction by Viollet-le-Duc

cut off from allies and their aid. Meanwhile, the enemy enlisted all means of siegecraft. Projectiles, usually large stones, were hurled by machines worked by tension, torsion or counterpoise. Even the strongest walls could be damaged by ramming. But most effort was expended upon forcing the main gate or getting inside the castle itself, either openly or secretly.

bringing down a wall by tunnelling

siege tower or belfry.
Wet hides protected the tower from burning. Archers gave supporting fire to the attackers

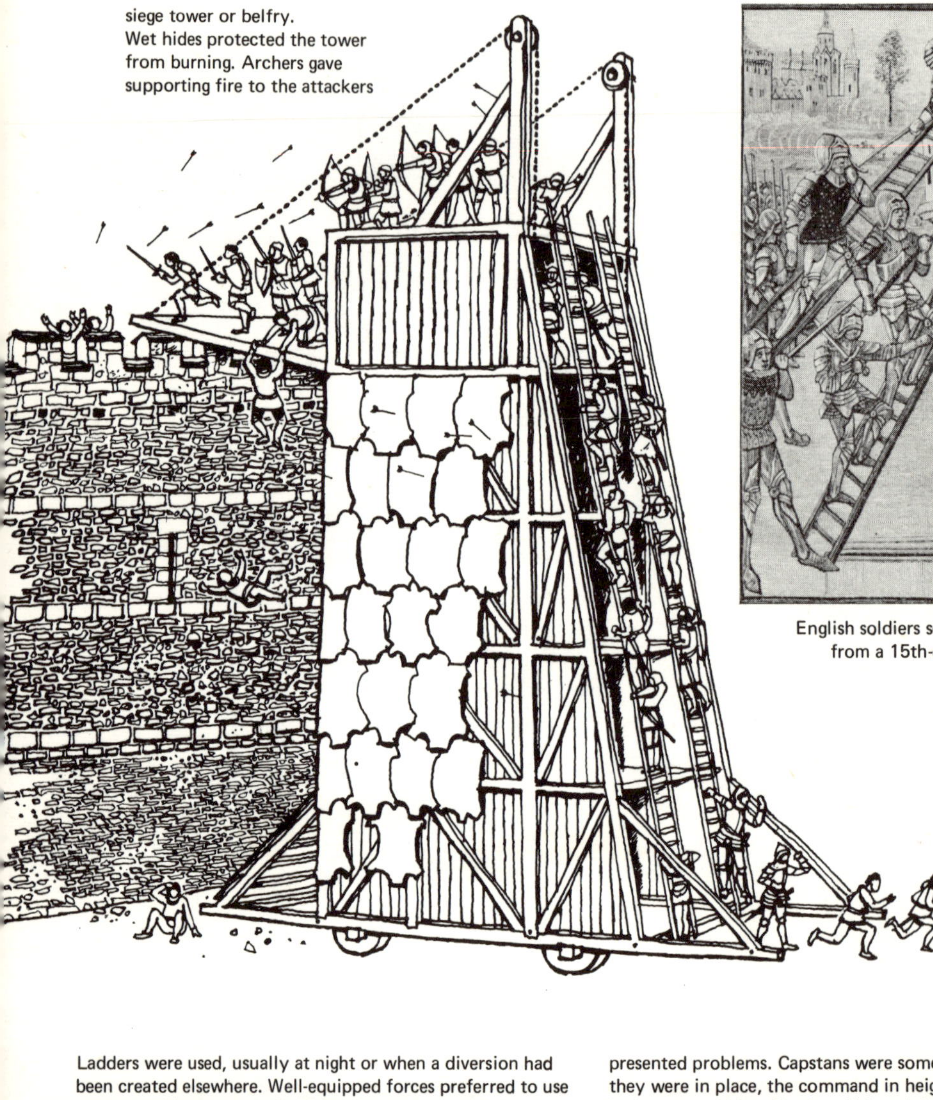

English soldiers scaling a fortress in Gasc
from a 15th-century Flemish manusc

Ladders were used, usually at night or when a diversion had been created elsewhere. Well-equipped forces preferred to use great movable towers, built higher than the castle walls, and fitted with a drawbridge. The movement of these siege towers presented problems. Capstans were sometimes used. Once they were in place, the command in height possessed by the besiegers could be effective. Although less effective against the immense stone walls of concentric castles, mining could

siege in classical times showing mining, a catapult and tower. The besiegers having raised a platform and built a wooden tower, have in turn successfully been undermined by the besieged, who are also using a mangonel

cross-section showing a double *corvus* or crane for breaking the blow of a battering-ram

siege, 15th century. Shows cannons, siege tower and ladder

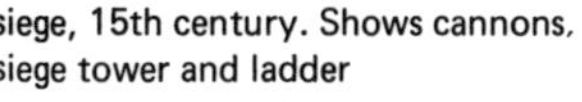

mangonel worked solely by torsion

still be an effective method of destroying the garrison's defence. Miners hollowed out large caverns, propping up the tunnels with timber. Cavern and tunnels were filled with straw, wooden faggots and animal fat. Ignited, the mass of inflammable material soon roared into flame. The props were burnt. The roofs of the tunnels collapsed, and brought down the wall. But the most effective method was the 'wooden horse' technique of getting besiegers into the castle.

Prisoners

◁ Carisbrooke Castle. Charles I imprisoned here in 1647

Castle Rising. Queen Isobel, wife of Edward II, imprisoned here for 21 years

Charles I

Berkeley Castle. Edward II imprisoned he in a dungeon through whic the castle sewer ra

Sir Walter Raleigh, imprisoned in the Tower of London

Edward II

Charles d'Orleans, prisoner in the White Tower, Tower of London

◁ the Castle of Chillon, Switzerland, used as a prison for François Bonivard, a hero of the Swiss Reformation who inspired Byron's poem, *The Prisoner of Chillon*

Lord Byron

The isolation and immense strength of the castle made it the perfect repository for prisoners. Every castle had its dungeons where prisoners could be incarcerated and tortured. The Tower of London is an historic State prison. The Bastille was the most loathed fortress in France until it was torn down by the revolutionaries. Byron's poem *The Prisoner of Chillon* describes the foul conditions in which castle prisoners were often kept.

Castel del Monte, Italy, c.1240, the most beautiful of many castles built by Frederick II, a patron of the arts; used chiefly as a hunting lodge

Civilization

Charlemagne finding the body of Roland with his sword Duvendal and his horn beside him, at Roncesvalles

Hall of the Singers or Sängersaal at Wartburg Castle

Duc de Berry, a Prince of France and patron of the arts, rides away with some of his courtiers from Château de Saumur. Pictures of the Duke's castles appear in the manuscript *Très Riches Heures* commissioned by him

Poets and chroniclers were drawn to the princely courts in the great castles for rewards and audience. It was therefore in the castle that European folk tales began. Troubadours sang lyrics in praise of the Virgin or recounted long epics telling of the deeds of valour of famous knights. The *Chansons de geste,* of which more than eighty survive, includes the story of Roland and Charlemagne. Arthurian legends may have been first told in castles.

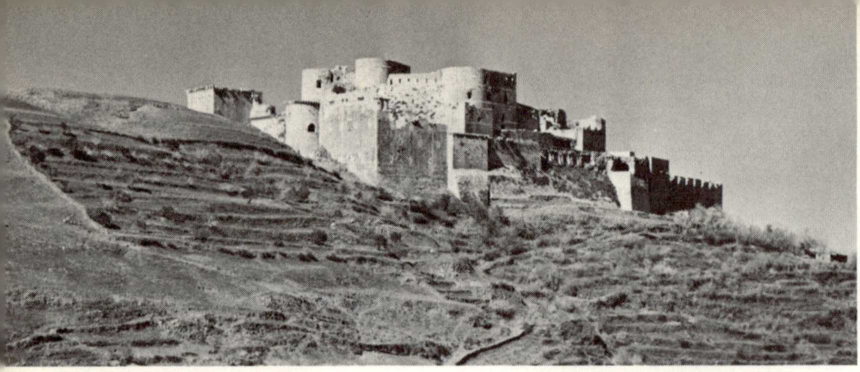

◁ Krak des Chevaliers

Crusader castles

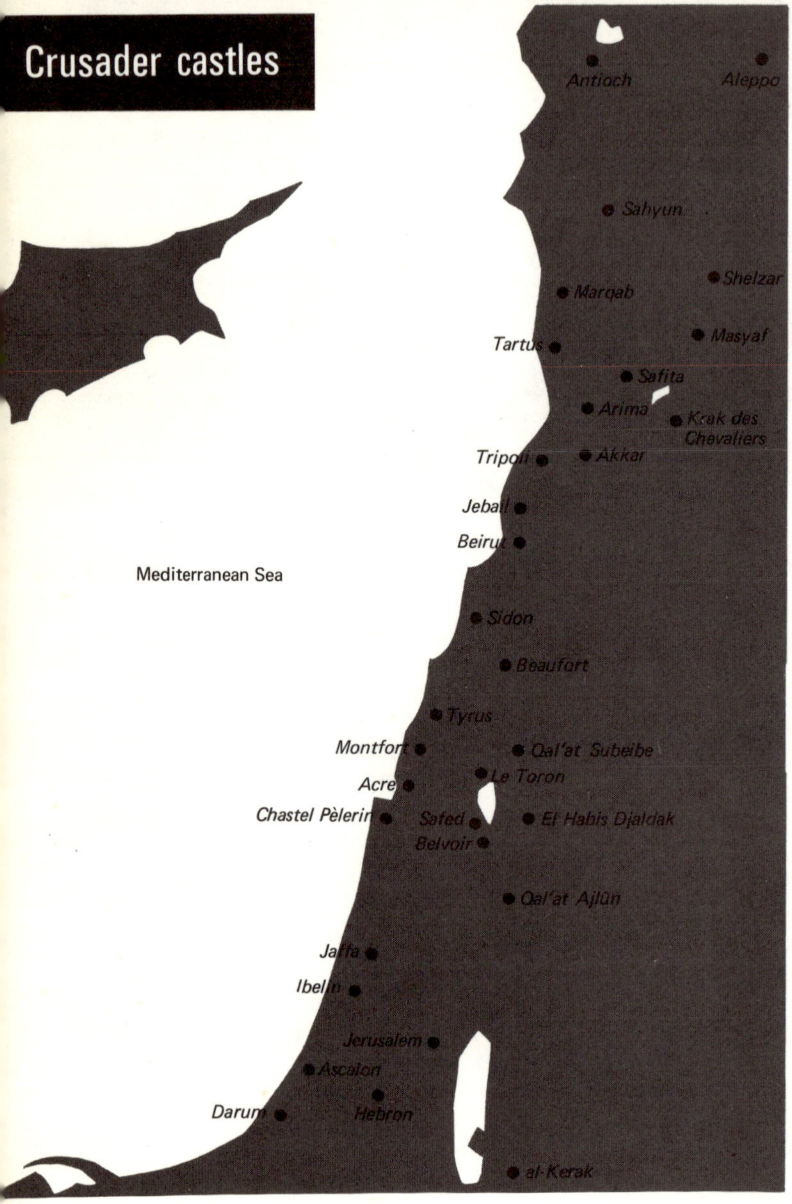

Antioch
Aleppo
Sahyun
Marqab
Shelzar
Tartus
Masyaf
Safita
Arima
Krak des Chevaliers
Tripoli
Akkar
Jebail
Beirut
Mediterranean Sea
Sidon
Beaufort
Tyrus
Montfort
Qal'at Subeibe
Le Toron
Acre
Chastel Pèlerin
Safed
El Habis Djaldak
Belvoir
Qal'at Ajlūn
Jaffa
Ibelin
Jerusalem
Ascalon
Darum
Hebron
al-Kerak

Crusader castles in the Levant

the vaulted passage known as the great ramp was the entrance to Krak. It was heavily fortified by machicolations, loopholes and portcullises. In fact, it was a barbican turned inwards ▽

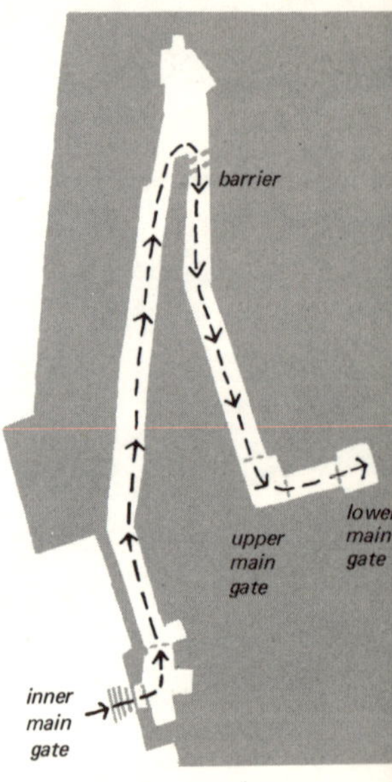

great ramp and entrance to Krak.

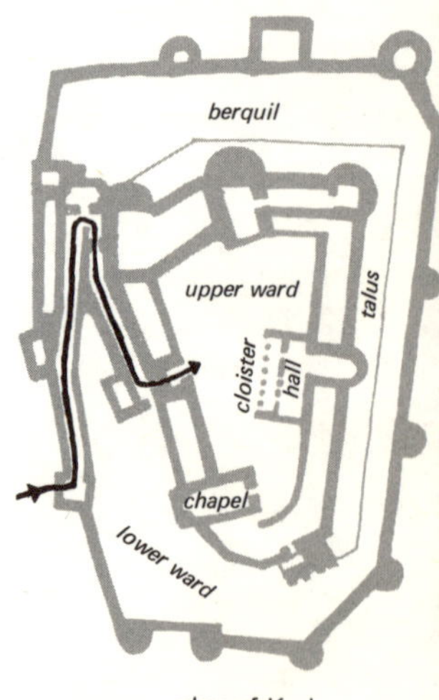

plan of Krak

The period during which the castle became a part of the European scene and then declined corresponds with the rise and fall of chivalry. Knightly chivalry expressed itself in the Crusades — the setting forth to do battle against the infidel, to defend the holy places, and to protect the pilgrim routes. The Crusades created three famous Orders. The Knights Hospitaller were founded in the eleventh century to succour sick pilgrims. It changed its character under the grand

ne of the great cellars at Krak. Soldiers could be quartered here and provisions stored. Light is provided by holes in the roof

cloister of the great hall at Krak with a group of Knights Hospitallers. European masons joined the Order and this is a fine example of their work

berquil or reservoir at Krak

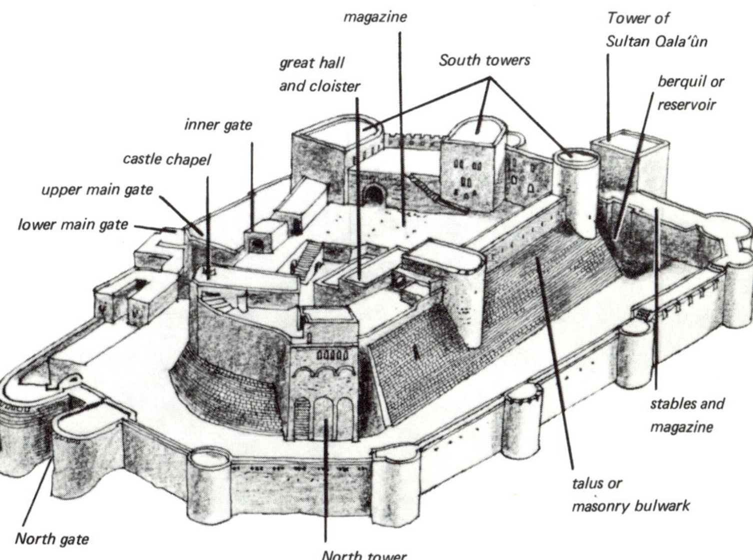

view of Krak showing the concentric defences

mastership of Raymond du Puy. The Knights Templar were also a military body answerable to the Church. The knights of both Orders were poor but their Orders were rich, and expanded in land dominated by Crusader castles. The third Crusader Order provided many of the finest castles. This was the Order of Teutonic Knights whose regions were known as the Ordensland. The original intention of the Crusader knights was to make Jerusalem and the Holy Land part of Europe.

Walled towns

△ Carcassonne Castle, France, most powerful concentric fortification of the medieval West. The huge Tour de la Vade, far right, is the strongest in the outer walls

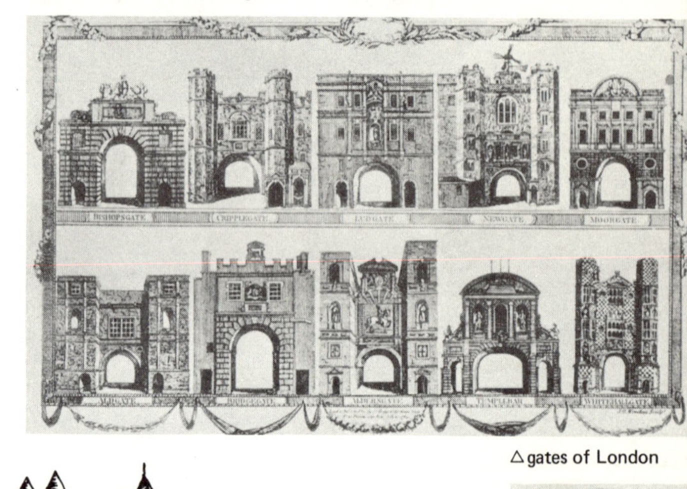

△ gates of London

portrait of Col. Eugène Viollet-le-Duc, French architect of the 1800s, who restored Carcasso

Carcassonne, France. Tour Carrée de l'Evêque and a sector of the walls near the cathedral. Reconstruction o possible scene in the Middle Ages

Medieval merchants and craftsmen created the towns of Europe. But they did not invent the idea of walled fortification that is so common to European medieval towns. A biblical story refers to the walls of Jericho. The walls of Babylon were one of the seven wonders of the world. The wall, with its guarded gates, was regarded as a necessity in turbulent medieval times. The town had to be kept secure against marauders, rebels and bands of mercenary soldiers

English artist's idea of Constantinople c.1340, and a group dancing to tabor and pipe

licklegate Bar, York

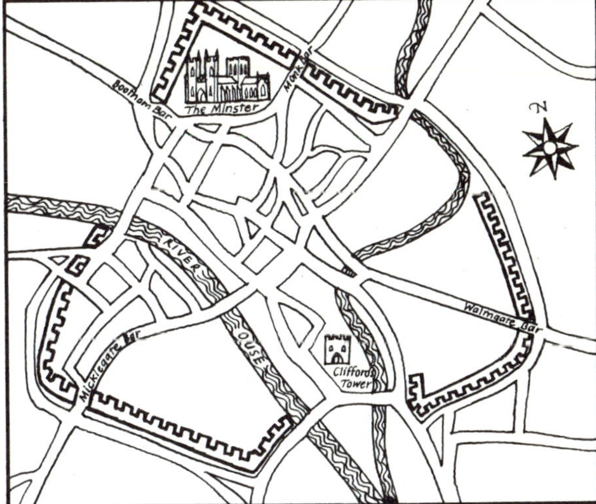

△ map of York, showing the walls running for a total of three miles. Dating from the time of Edward III. The Minster, Clifford's Tower, mid-13th century, and the famous bars or gates

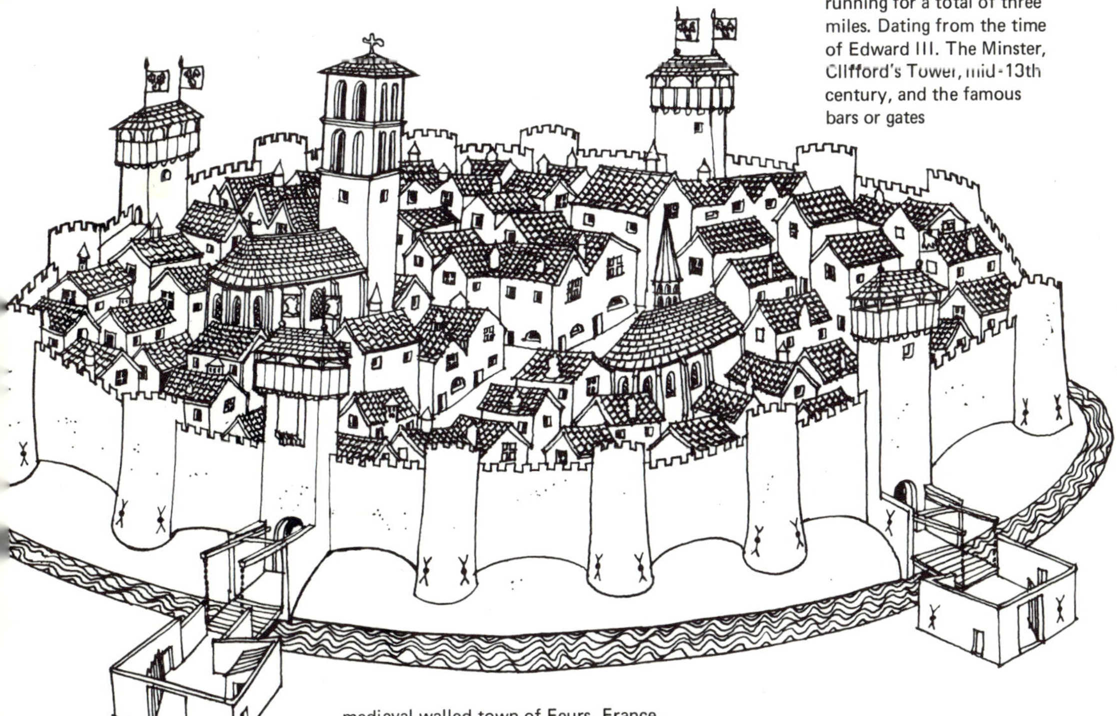

medieval walled town of Feurs, France. Note the barbicans, drawbridges and moat and the machicolations above the entrance gates

returning from the wars. Burghers raised their own militia, and spent as much as three-quarters of their revenue for defence. Not only have these fortifications withstood the onslaught of attackers intent on the sack and pillage of the town, but many of them have withstood the ravages of time. The great walls of Constantinople were unbreached for 1000 years. When the Turks smashed their way through in 1453, the whole of European civilization was at risk.

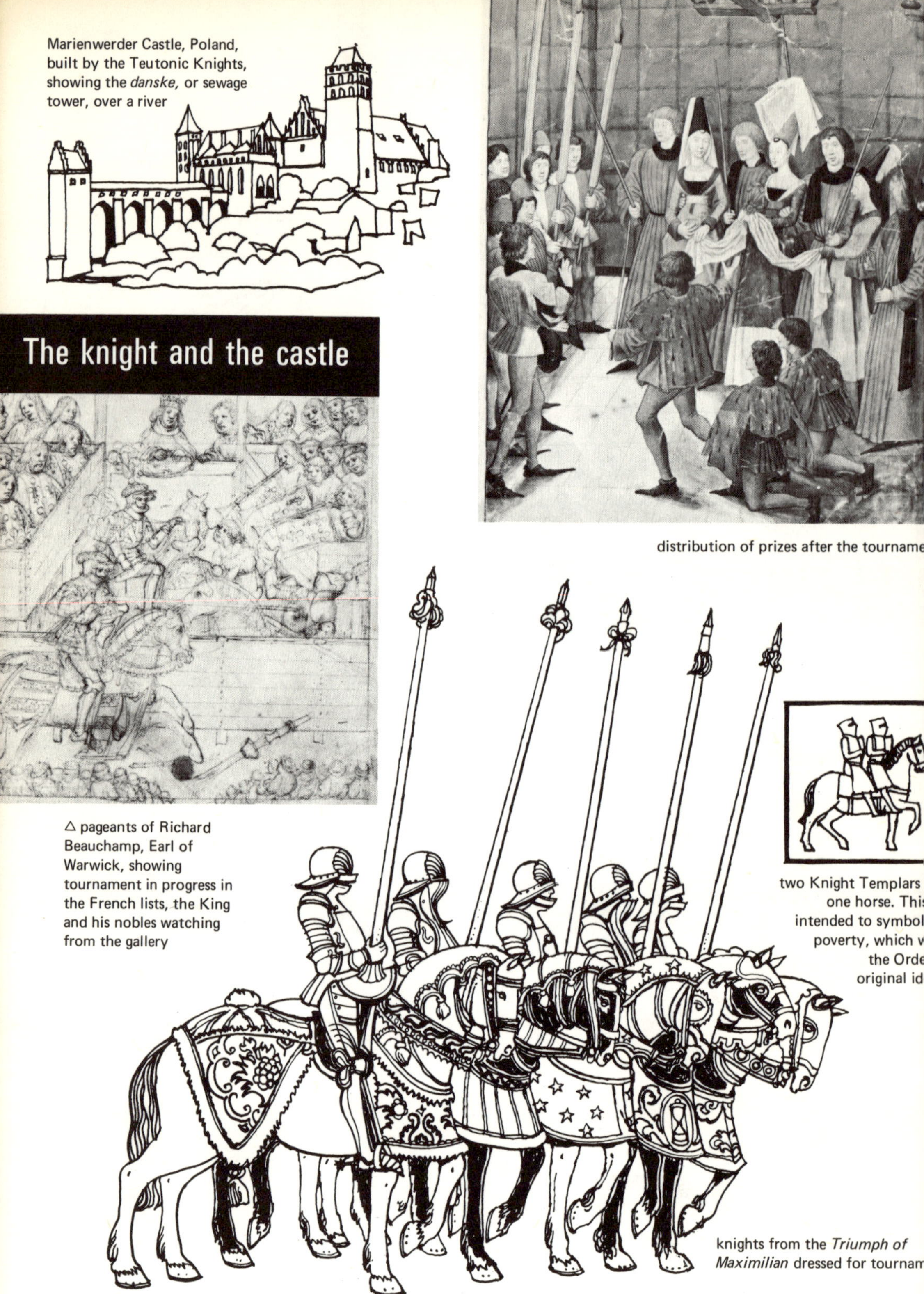

Marienwerder Castle, Poland, built by the Teutonic Knights, showing the *danske,* or sewage tower, over a river

The knight and the castle

distribution of prizes after the tourname

△ pageants of Richard Beauchamp, Earl of Warwick, showing tournament in progress in the French lists, the King and his nobles watching from the gallery

two Knight Templars
one horse. This
intended to symbol
poverty, which w
the Orde
original id

knights from the *Triumph of Maximilian* dressed for tournam

In the feudal system, every landowner had military obligations, either to the king or to his overlord. He was contracted to provide a stated number of knights and soldiers to put down rebellions, repel foreign invasion, provide garrisons for castles or engage in private wars or sieges. A large part of his education was therefore concentrated upon preparation for battle. The castle was a backcloth to the tournament, and also a base for training.

) at Gravensteen Castle, Belgium

astles and trade

view of the town of Ghent from the keep of Gravensteen. This epitomises the confrontation of the military stronghold of the aristocratic family with the houses and great churches of the prosperous trading city

vnsmen receiving their
'’s charter from their
al feudal lord

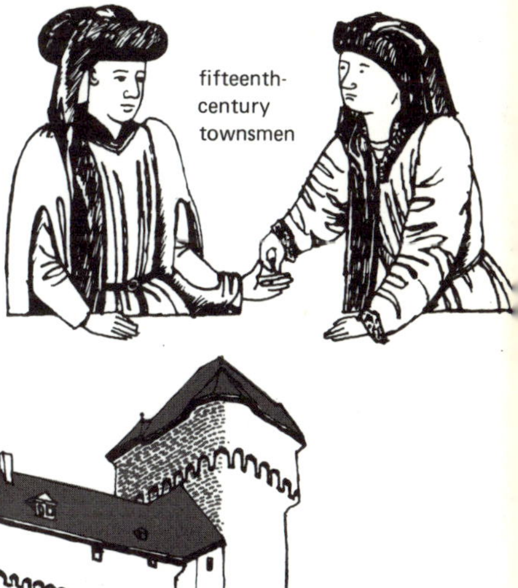

fifteenth-century townsmen

feature of German castles, the Bergfried or tower. Marksburg, the best preserved of the Rhine castles. These castles levied tolls from traders using the river

As the wars of the Middle Ages abated, more towns were established. Roads linked the towns, and trade and traffic increased. The landowners, who owned the land the merchants had to cross, found a growing source of revenue through tolls and taxes. The river Rhine, an historic trade route, at one time had more than sixty castles exacting toll from merchants. During the 13th century towns formed leagues to fight this imposition.

The decline of the castle

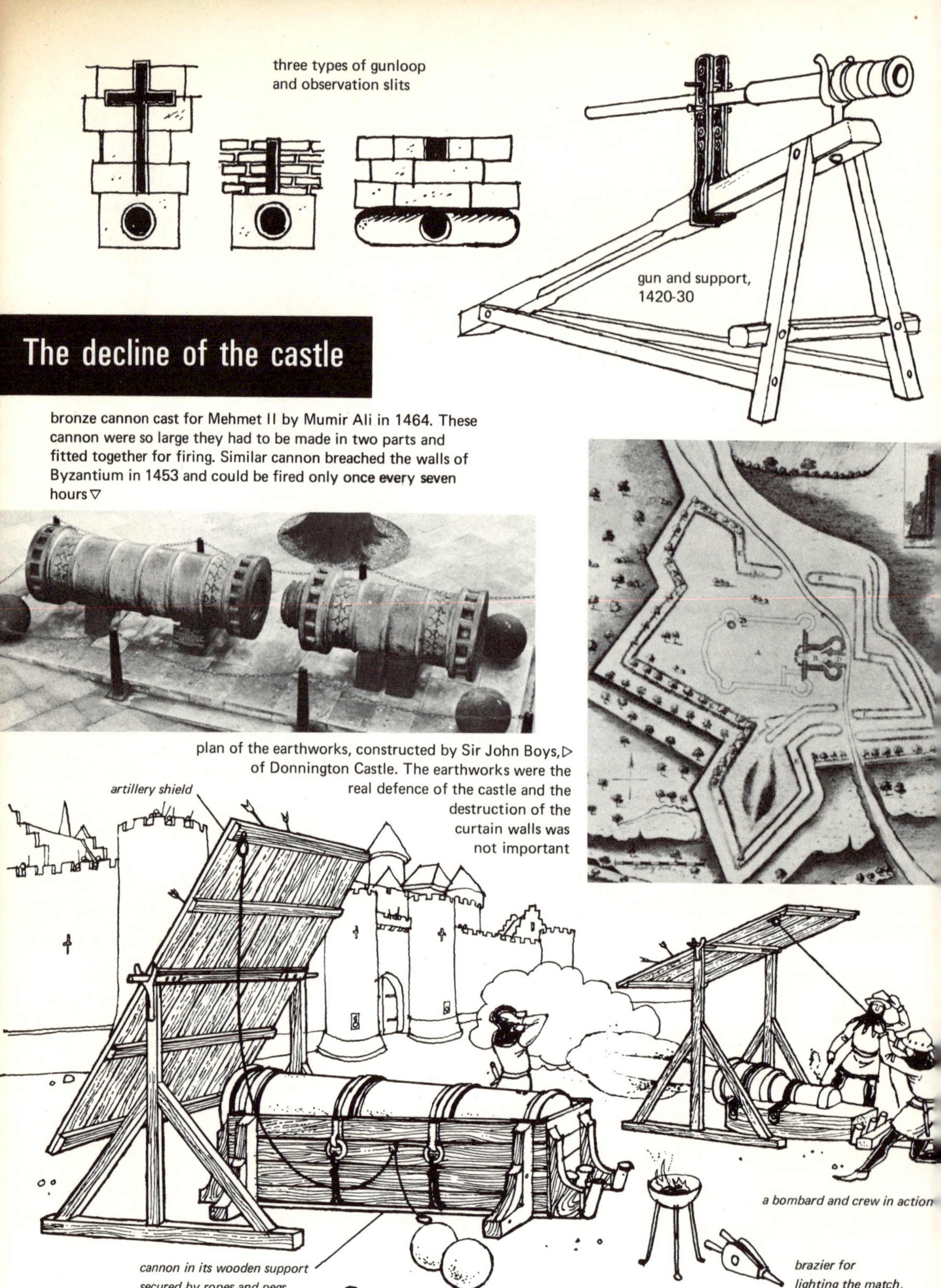

three types of gunloop and observation slits

gun and support, 1420-30

bronze cannon cast for Mehmet II by Mumir Ali in 1464. These cannon were so large they had to be made in two parts and fitted together for firing. Similar cannon breached the walls of Byzantium in 1453 and could be fired only once every seven hours ▽

plan of the earthworks, constructed by Sir John Boys, ▷ of Donnington Castle. The earthworks were the real defence of the castle and the destruction of the curtain walls was not important

a bombard and crew in action

Throughout the 13th and 14th centuries the castle grew in power and strength, until, against the normal medieval attack, it was well-nigh impregnable. But gunpowder and cannon pounded the castle into inevitable decay. At first artillery was welcomed by the defenders of castles. During the next century, however, cannons grew in power and effect, and blasted the castle walls. By the 17th century the castle was outdated, and a candidate for the guide-books.